The Cambrian Coast 2
Harlech to Aberystwyth explored

Gwasg Carreg Gwalch

First published in 2022
© publication: Gwasg Carreg Gwalch 2022

ISBN: 978-1-84524-245-9

Cover design: Eleri Owen
Map: Alison Davies

Published by Gwasg Carreg Gwalch,
12 Iard yr Orsaf, Llanrwst, Wales LL26 0EH
tel: 01492 642031
email: llanrwst@carreg-gwalch.cymru
website: www.carreg-gwalch.cymru

Image Sources

The publishers wish to gratefully acknowledge
all assistance in obtaining permission to
reproduce images from the following sources:

Visit Wales (crown copyright)
1, 2, 11b, 15, 17, 31, 34b, 39, 45, 47, 50, 51, 54, 64,
65, 66b, 69, 71, 81, 82, 84, 85, 87, 90b,c

Wikimedia Commons
4, 5, 19b

Keith Morris
9, 55

Aberystwyth lights

Contents

Harlech–Aberystwyth

'*Cambria*' was what the Romans called *Cymru* (Wales), and 'Cambrian Coast' has no clearly defined limits. Does it include the whole coastline of the country, from Prestatyn to the Severn Bridge? Is it just the western seaboard, linking the peninsulas of Llŷn in the north and Pembrokeshire in the south? To most people it is neither of these, but is identified with the Cambrian Coast Railway and its two branches connecting Pwllheli and Aberystwyth. During its 150-year history this line has survived the Beeching axe and other bureaucratic threats, and continues to provide one of the most picturesque train journeys you will find anywhere.

This book is not just about the railway, but covers an area loosely based on the southern section of the line, from Aberystwyth to Harlech. With the sea on one side and the hills and mountains of Snowdonia National Park on the other, the train winds its way through a remarkable variety of landscapes and communities. We sometimes take a detour from the railway to the slate quarries, market towns and harsher climate further inland.

Whether you explore the area by rail, by car, on your bike or on foot, the book will guide you through some of the place-names, history and culture of the area, and introduce some of the people and events that left their marks on the landscape.

Another volume in the series continue the journey northwards from Harlech to Pwllheli.

CADER IDRIS & THE AFON MAWDDACH

GWR **WALES** GWR

Early rail posters along the Cambrian Coast railway

HARLECH CASTLE
MERIONETH

Open to the public all the year round. Weekdays at 9.30 a.m.
Sundays 2 p.m. Admission: Adults 1/-. Children under 14 years 6d.

BY TRAIN TO HARLECH STATION
which is in close proximity to the Castle

WESTERN REGION

ABERYSTWYTH

Illustrated Booklet free from
Bureau Manager. "Sea Pearl". Aberystwyth.

GWR

Harlech
Llanfair
Slate Caverns
Rhinog Fawr 720m
RHINOG
Rhinog Fach 712m
Llanbedr
Cwm Nantcol
Sarn Badrig
Y Llethr 754m
GWYNEDD
A470
A494
Cambrian Coast Railway
Dyffryn Ardudwy
Ysgethin
Diffwys 750m
GWYDD
Llanddwywe
Tal-y-bont
Bont-ddu
Mawddach
A496
Llanaber
Penmaenpool
Dolgellau
A470
Bermo (Barmouth)
A493
Llynnau Cregennen
Fairbourne Railway
Arthog
Cader Idris 892m
Llwyngwril
Llyn Myngul
Castell y Bere
A487
Corris
Corris Craft Centre
Corris Railway
A470
Llangelynnin
Dysynni
B4405
Llanegryn
Abergynolwyn
Centre for Alternative Technology
Dyfi
Bae Ceredigion
Bryncrug
Tal-y-llyn Railway
Machynlleth
Tywyn
Pennal
Owain Glyndŵr's Parliament House
Derwen-las
POWYS
A493
Dyfi Junction
Aberdyfi (Aberdovey)
Ffwrnais
A487
Ynys-las
B4353
Cambrian Coast Railway
Tre Taliesin
Borth
Tal-y-bont
B4572
Sarn Gynfelyn
CEREDIGION
Bow Street
Clarach
Penrhyn-coch
A4159
Ponterwyd
A44
Aberystwyth
Llanbadarn Fawr
A44
A487
Capel Bangor
Vale of Rheidol Narrow Gauge Railway
Rheidol
Pontarfynach (Devil's Bridge)
A4120

miles 5
0
kilometres 10
0
Contains Ordnance Survey data
© Crown copyright and database right 2016

Harlech to Barmouth (Bermo)

Ancient Stones

Stones are an essential element of Ardudwy and parts of the landscape are reminiscent of Conamara and western Ireland. The fields are separated by sturdy high stone walls, the result of hard labour at the time of the land enclosures some two or three centuries ago.

In Bwlch Tyddiad, the so-called 'Roman Steps', follow a prehistoric path climbing from Cwm Bychan in Ardudwy through a gap in the Rhinogydd towards the east. At some point – possibly during the era of the packhorse in the Middle Ages – stone steps were placed along the path, to make it easier for horses to cross from Harlech to the Trawsfynydd valley. There are very few Roman remains in

Stone walls near Llanaber

Ardudwy – overland routes were fundamental to their empire and the Romans would have considered the area to the west of the Rhinogydd as being inaccessible.

The Bwlch Tyddiad steps are only one of a number of ancient tracks which lead from the coast through the hills – evidence of how successive waves of migrants and visitors have made landfall on this coast from the New Stone Age onwards.

There are six cromlechs (*dolmens*) dating back to about 2500 BC within a five mile radius of Harlech. These are portal cromlechs and the two most notable examples are to be found behind the school in Dyffryn Ardudwy. The two now stand separately but the remains of the large earth mound nearby suggest that they were originally part of a single memorial. The cromlechs consist of two huge stones facing each other, forming a gateway surmounted by a slanting capstone. As is usual with such designs, the gateway was closed symbolically with a slightly smaller stone.

The capstones are smooth and flat underneath and rough and convex on the upper side, suggesting that the underside was visible to those entering the burial chamber but that the upper surface was covered by a mound of stones and earth.

Only fragments of the cromlechs remain – traces of an ancient culture about which we now know very little. The stone in Llanbedr church is inscribed with a remarkable spiral pattern which is also to be found in Ireland and Malta and at several other ancient sites.

The Dyffryn Ardudwy cromlechs

The prehistoric path at Bwlch Tyddiad

The Celtic Church and the Meirionnydd coast

The ancient church of *Bermo* (Barmouth), known as Llanaber, is situated to the north of the present-day town on the high ground above the spot where Afon Mawddach (*afon*: river) formerly flowed into the sea. The church was originally consecrated to one of the old Welsh saints, Bodfan, who was a missionary in Ardudwy in the golden age of the Celtic Church. Christianity came to Wales during the Roman period when the Welsh saints established *llannau* (churches) and made contact with their fellow Celts in Ireland, Cornwall and Brittany a century before Saint Augustine arrived in England to spread the gospel among the pagans there.

The architecture of the ancient church at Llanaber today dates from the thirteenth century and it is now consecrated to the Virgin Mary. In the church, the two memorial stones dating from the 5th to the 7th centuries commemorate the early Christians who moved here from Brittany. The church faces Bae Ceredigion and the westerly island of *Enlli* (Bardsey), that lies just off Llŷn – the bodies of the saints would be carried by boat to be buried on the island during this early period.

There are three other churches in Barmouth – the Catholic Church, which is consecrated to Tudwal, another of the saints of these shores; the beautiful church of John the Evangelist, dating from 1889, and the church of Dewi Sant (St David) near the harbour. This simple church was built in 1830 on the site of an old shipbuilding yard; it was used mainly by sailors to pray for safety on the sea and to give thanks for a safe passage after coming home. The 'mariners' church' is a familiar institution in several Celtic ports – they are also to be seen in Brittany and Cornwall.

Another church with an obvious maritime connection is Llandanwg, in the sand-dunes below Llanfair near Harlech. Tanwg was a member of Cadfan Sant's retinue, who came to this coast from Brittany. Cadfan established his mother church at Tywyn and the rest of his retinue went to other parts of Meirionnydd – Tanwg came to Llandanwg; Enddwyn to

1. Llanaber church; 2. St Tudwal's church at Barmouth; 3. The harbour church in Barmouth.

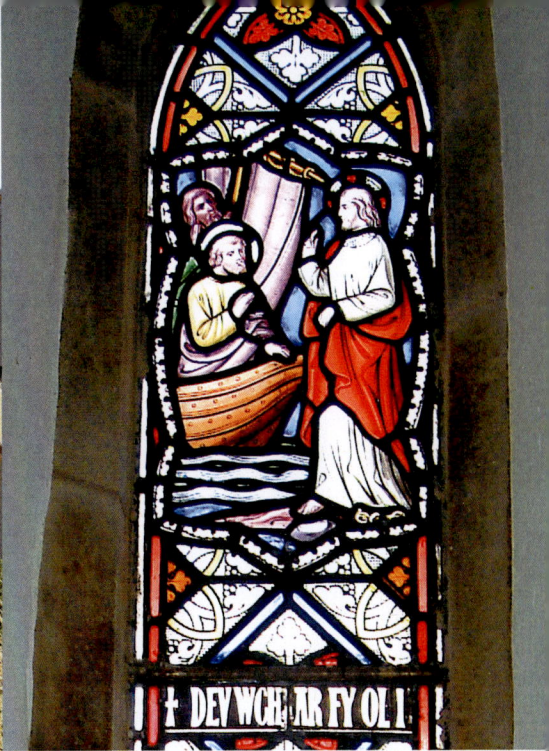

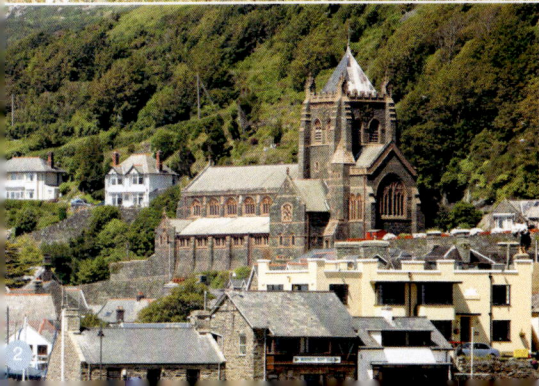

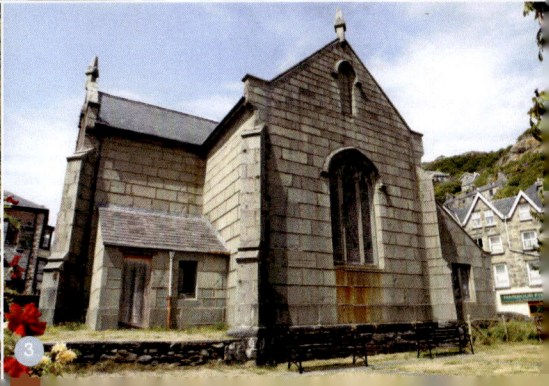

Llanenddwyn, near Dyffryn Ardudwy; Dwywe to Llanddwywe near Tal-y-bont and Tegwyn to Llandecwyn a few miles north-east of Harlech.

In a terrible storm in the nineteenth century, the sea smashed the wall of Llandanwg cemetery and the gravestones were buried under great mounds of sand. Most of the gravestones were saved and the church was cleared of sand after that, but it stands today enclosed by the sand-dunes. One of the graves under the eastern window of the church is inscribed with the letters 'I.Ph'. This is believed to be the grave of Siôn Phylip of Mochras, a renowned 16th century poet from Ardudwy.

Llanenddwyn is the only cruciform church in Ardudwy and in Llanddwywe, the date of the church's construction, 1593, is to be found on the southern entrance. The Corsygedol family chapel stands on the northern side with a large screen between it and the nave of the church.

1. Llandanwg church; 2. in Llanbedr church; 3. Llanddwywe church.

Aber Mawddach

Despite its comparatively short length Afon Mawddach is endowed with a fine estuary. It springs from the wild moors between Trawsfynydd and Bala and carries with it the metallic hues of the rocks as it flows down the dramatic river valley. It follows the mountains to the sea and the wooded slopes, rocky peaks and the expansive sandbanks of the estuary combine to create a remarkably attractive vista.

At one time, the river flowed to the sea over the low-lying ground where today are situated Barmouth's high street and dwellings. In the Middle Ages, a small settlement was established on the slopes of the northern spit of the estuary – Llanaber – the site of the old parish church to this day. Later, cottages were built on the cliff face at Barmouth – this is the oldest part of the town and it is built on a series of rock terraces, the threshold of one house being located behind the chimney pot of the one in front of it, and an intriguing network of steep paths winds between them. It is worth going for a stroll along these paths to see the craftsmanship of the old stonemasons juxtaposed with the colourful flowers of the rocky gardens.

Over the centuries, the sand-banks have spread across the estuary blocking the original entrance. By now a ridge of sand connects the reed-covered, shingle of Ynys y Brawd (*the friar's island*) at the mouth of the harbour to the mainland, and Afon Mawddach has carved a new channel for itself to the sea.

When Gerallt Gymro and Bishop Baldwin came on their famous journey through Wales in search of volunteers to fight in the third Crusade in 1188, they were rowed across the Mawddach estuary – there must have been a ferry service there since time immemorial for travellers between Gwynedd and Deheubarth (*southern Wales*). In the 15th century there was a plan to land an army from Scotland at Barmouth to support Owain Glyndŵr's rebellion.

In 1565, a report was commissioned on the ports and harbours of Meirionnydd, in response to Elizabeth I's concern that this coastline was swarming with pirates – and the queen of England certainly knew a thing or two about piracy! According to this report. there were at that time four houses and two ferries at Barmouth, and herring was the staple diet of the inhabitants. By 1587 the little port had its own ship – *L'Ange de Bermo* – which imported corn mainly for the local market. There were big changes afoot, however, and with its westerly location facing the New World, Barmouth would grow during the next two centuries to become one of Wales' most important ports with worldwide connections.

Aber Mawddach

A Norman Castle

After centuries of sustained resistance, the military capability of the Welsh eventually succumbed to one of the most costly invasions of the Middle Ages in 1282-3. Edward I – the king of England at the time – was one of the greediest and most merciless monarchs of his age and through a combination of a strong naval force, mercenaries from every corner of Europe and a huge fund of money, he succeeded in conquering the north-west, and in overwintering there. When Llywelyn ap Gruffudd, the leader of the Welsh, was killed in an ambush at Cilmeri in 1282, the Welsh lost their prince and the will to fight to safeguard their identity.

It was a superficial victory for the foreign army however. It soon became obvious to Edward that he would have to prepare for the next rebellion by the Welsh. This was achieved by building a chain of huge castles around the heartland of *Eryri* (Snowdonia). This was the costliest scheme of its kind in Europe during the Middle Ages – a manifestation of the danger which Edward still perceived as being posed by the Welsh.

Harlech was the southernmost of those castles. There had originally been a Welsh castle there but any remains thereof were destroyed by the king of England's designer, James St George of Savoy in France. St George had already won acclaim as a military architect and he followed Edward to Wales to supervise the work of erecting strong, new fortifications at Conwy, Caernarfon, Harlech and Biwmares. They were built for warfare, and are situated close to the sea to facilitate their supply in times of crisis, and are strategically located in a powerful position from which to challenge the hinterland.

All the Edwardian castles have a unique character and Harlech is no exception: from the outside it has a striking and powerful appearance, standing shoulder to shoulder with the peaks of Snowdonia, but inside it is more homely and compact. It has the same atmosphere as a large mansion, with rather a neat courtyard and fine windows in its inner walls – a castle which could also serve as a family residence.

Harlech castle was completed in 1290,

Harlech castle

in good time to withstand the great Welsh uprising of 1294-5 under the leadership of Madog ap Llywelyn. At that time, the sea and maritime support was key to the garrison's ability to hold their ground in the face of incursions by the Welsh.

In contrast to the other castles, Edward did not establish a borough in the shadow of Harlech castle to attract merchants and foreign government officials to colonise the country. No privileged town was created here to oppress the Welsh, but that did not prevent Welsh forces from attacking the castle once again during another rebellion in 1400.

The Home of Owain Glyndŵr

It is ironic that the most famous person ever to make his home in Harlech castle was the Welsh national hero Owain Glyndŵr. It was obvious that he too had an eye for a favourable site.

Wales had suffered more than a century of barbaric government in the shadow of Edward I's castles and towns. A huge number of men and boys had been killed as a precaution in case of rebellion and according to English records, hundreds more women, children and old people were also slaughtered. After 1282, taxes in Wales increased by six hundred per cent – the English crown was bankrupt after the costly war. Then, the first anti-Welsh laws were passed – the Welsh could neither hold office nor possess land in a town nor trade beyond the walls of a town; they were not allowed to carry arms and unable to accuse an Englishman of committing any offence; *Cymraeg* (the Welsh language) was forbidden as a public language and a Welshman could be executed without the sanction of a court of law if he were caught in a town after nightfall.

Six hundred years ago, the Welsh had had enough of this racial oppression. Owain of Glyndyfrdwy, which lies to the south of Rhuthun, rose up as a leader and together with three hundred followers, attacked the town of Rhuthun and razed it to the ground in September 1400. Over the years that followed every English town in Wales was attacked and burnt; many of the 'castles of conquest' were attacked too, several even being successfully captured.

One of the castles which fell into the hands of Glyndŵr's army in the spring of 1404 was Harlech. He moved his headquarters and family there, and for four years this had a very positive effect on his campaign. During that period Glyndŵr received a number of European ambassadors at Harlech and in 1405 and 1406, a Welsh *senedd* (parliament) was held there three times.

A large English army of some one thousand men, arrived to besiege Harlech castle in 1408. It was a long siege throughout the spring and summer and was met by staunch Welsh resistance. Traces of the prolonged bombardment are still to be seen on the defences, which resulted in the castle's evacuation in February 1409. Marged, Owain's wife and Catrin, his daughter and her children were

An enamel
a horse harne...
Castle. It bears th...
Glyndŵr as Prince of ...
piece of concrete evidence f...

An enamelled martingale bearing the arms of Owain Glyndŵr found at Harlech

The royal seal of Owain Glyndŵr

taken to the Tower of London but Owain himself managed to escape.

After the promise of Glyndŵr's ascendancy, when the foundations of modern Wales were laid in both word and deed, Glyndŵr's fortunes started to ebb. He was under constant pressure from the English armies and the country became gravely impoverished as a result of the continuing state of war. After fifteen years of rebellion, Owain and his small band of faithful followers disappeared from the history books to the world of mythology. It is not known where he died, but his great dream of Wales enjoying full national status amongst the countries of Europe, lives on.

The Gentry Houses of Ardudwy

As Glyndŵr's story became legend, the responsibility for defending different areas of Wales from the oppressive English penal laws fell to the gentry. Various families from the great houses of Ardudwy – Maes-y-neuadd, Cwm Bychan, Corsygedol and others, were descendants of the old Welsh princes. They maintained the traditional role of the Welsh gentry – defending their land and people and providing patronage for the poets and local culture.

In the 15th century, the Welsh were looking for a national leader to succeed Glyndŵr. People started to whisper the name of Harri, one of the descendants of the Tudur family from Penmynydd, *Môn* (Anglesey), who was in exile in Brittany, but through his grandfather's marriage could claim succession to the English throne through the House of Lancaster. Sometime between 1460 and 1485, the period of the Wars of the Roses, Gruffudd Fychan, Corsygedol, built a house on the edge of the Mawddach estuary, Tŷ Gwyn (*white house*) at Barmouth, which has been restored and its upper floor recently turned into a museum. According to tradition, Jasper Tudur, Harri Tudur's uncle, sailed here and met with the gentry of the area at Tŷ Gwyn in order to gain support for the rebellion. There was talk that Harri would land his Breton army on the shores of the Mawddach estuary and march to Bosworth Field from there, but eventually it was the harbour at Milford Haven which was chosen by the Tudors. Tŷ Gwyn was a popular sailors' tavern throughout the golden age of the port and you can still enjoy a meal and slake your thirst downstairs, experiencing the atmosphere of the old days.

The Welsh gentry gave their support to the victorious Harri Tudur, but having attained the throne in London, the king disregarded the needs of his fellow Welsh to a large extent. Some of the gentry became quite Anglicised in their language and ways, going to live in London and forgetting about their people back home. Others stayed true to the dreams of the Welsh.

One of these was General Henry Lloyd, Cwm Bychan, one of the Llwyd family, who was descended from the Welsh princes of Powys. He saw an opportunity to strike a blow against the English crown

Corsygedol

in his support for the Jacobeans. He went to France, became involved with the Irish Brigade who supported any enemy of England and joined the Jacobean rebellion in 1745.

Ellis Wynne was one of the Wynn family from Maes-y-neuadd on his mother's side. He inherited the mansion of Y Lasynys near Harlech and became the rector of Llandanwg parish in 1704. He was the author of a work of colourful prose which satirises sinners on their way to hell, and is one of the great classics of Welsh literature. Maes-y-neuadd is now a luxurious hotel and restaurant and Y Lasynys belongs to a local trust, who have restored it to its former glory and opened its doors to the public.

The Drovers' Roads

From the end of the Middle Ages until the arrival of the railways, the Welsh *porthmyn* (drovers) would drive thousands of cattle, sheep, pigs and geese each year from the mountain pastures to the rich grasslands of south-east England to be fattened up for the markets there. This was a journey of hundreds of miles, often over rough, and remote highland terrain. Amongst the dangers were wolves, highwaymen as well as severe weather conditions. Wales had its Wild West and its heroes on the droving trails long before Hollywood romanticised the cowboys of the New World.

The slopes, mountains and river valleys of Ardudwy were ideal for rearing good stock. The drovers would be local men, since the farmers were entrusting them with responsibility for their livestock throughout the journey. Each droving expedition contained an element of financial risk and investment. Blacksmiths were paid to shoe the cattle and sheep and for putting leather shoes or tar and sand on the feet of the geese before driving them over the mountains. At their journey's end, the drovers would be at the mercy of the marketplace and were responsible for ensuring the safe delivery of money back to Ardudwy which would be needed to support the local economy for another year. It is hardly surprising that the drovers were referred to as the 'Welsh Armada'.

No one had a right to a droving licence unless they were over 30 years old, married and a house owner. The drover himself would travel on horseback – but it was a different story for the other cattle hands – the rather tough and violent men and young lads who would be in charge of the herd or flock. These had a bad reputation for being rather too fond of their beer, feats of strength, fighting, wrestling and womanising as they moved from place to place on their journey. It is said that English publicans used to remove the curtains from the windows and take up the carpets when they heard that the Welsh drovers were on their way!

The droving centres in Ardudwy were Llanfair, Llanbedr and Tal-y-bont – there are gravestones in the sandy churchyard of Llandanwg for the Roberts family, famous

An old drovers' inn at Pontfadog

drovers of the area. Other notable drovers were the Puws of Llanfair.

Several place names record the drovers' trail through the mountain passes – the steep climb through Bwlch y Rhiwgyr, and the old inn of Llety Lloegr (*England's rest*) – the last refuge for the drovers before crossing the mountains for England), where the herds used to be shoed. The remains of their tracks can be seen winding up the slopes and ruins of the old drovers' taverns are to be found here and there on the mountainsides and an occasional wild pine by the side of the cart-tracks marking their route across the bare terrain.

The Rhinogydd range that the drovers had to climb

The Port of Barmouth

One of the main reasons for the prosperity of the port of Barmouth was the development of the wool industry. This was the most important industry in Meirionnydd, with weavers making cloth in their cottages and an increasing number of woollen mills being built. Until 1770, most of the produce from the rural valleys would go to the weekly market at Shrewsbury. The English monopoly was broken and in 1772, a depot was established in Barmouth for the long, white cloth known as *gweoedd* (webs), from where it was exported to several parts of the world – including Europe, North America and Mexico.

Meirionnydd's woollen mills produced rough flannels from the fleece of mountain sheep and after mixing it with the fleece of sheep from abroad, this was mainly sold as clothing for slaves in North and South America and the Caribbean. Ships would sail regularly from Barmouth across the Atlantic to the ports of Charleston and New Orleans, both centres of slavery.

Oak from the slopes of the Mawddach valley was especially suitable for shipbuilding which grew to be an important industry on the banks of the river. Between 1750 and 1865, a total of 318 ships were built along the Mawddach estuary, as far inland as Llanelltyd – many of them of a considerable size. With the development of the slate industry in Snowdonia, there was an increasing demand for even more ships. The golden age lasted until the 1860s when the railway reached the town.

The port of Barmouth was dredged in 1797 and 200 local merchants invested in undertaking to make the harbour safer and more accessible. Nowadays, only a handful of fishing boats and pleasure craft are left to lay claim to the old connection with the sea.

Several of the buildings in the vicinity of the old harbour have their own story. Among them is the Seamen's Mission – a zinc hut which was erected next to the railway bridge in 1890 to offer shelter and comfort to sailors who called in on their journey. This is the only one of its kind to have survived in Wales and it was restored in 1984. It is open to the public, and it

1. The fishermen's sculpture;
2. The Seamen's Mission; 3. Tŷ Gwyn.

1

2

3

contains an exhibition of old pictures and newspaper cuttings and a billiards room.

Also by the harbour is Hen Dŷ Crwn (*old roundhouse*). Its stone walls are two feet thick and the chimney which rises from the middle of the steep-slanting slate roof is purely ornamental. It was decided to erect the roundhouse in 1834 because respectable people of the town were concerned about the behaviour of an increasing number of drunken sailors in the port. Inside Tŷ Crwn there are two cells, one for men and the other for women, and an outer door to each. Drunks would be kept there overnight until they had sobered up sufficiently to appear before the magistrates' bench. When the police station was opened in the town in 1861, the building was no longer needed but it has been restored, and it now receives the attention it deserves as part of the harbour's heritage.

Shipwrecks and Rescues

Under the sea to the west of Harlech and Barmouth lie lowlands which were submerged at the end of the Ice Age. A folk memory has been preserved concerning this event in the old legend of Cantre'r Gwaelod (*the lowland hundred*) and the remains of tree-roots which appear at low tide give credence to the story. Also at low tide Sarn Badrig (*Patricks' causeway*) can be seen. This is an extended rocky ridge under the sea stretching for miles towards the south-west of Ynys Fochras. This, according to the legend, was one of the dykes of Cantre'r Gwaelod. The causeway was a nightmare for sailors and several ships have foundered on it over the centuries.

At the end of the 1970s, divers discovered the remains of two vessels, one on top of the other, some five miles to the north of Barmouth. It is believed that they were wrecked on Sarn Badrig in a great storm over 200 years ago. The bell from one of the ships was raised from the seabed and it was found to date from 1677. It was carrying a cargo of marble from the

Hen Dŷ Crwn at Barmouth

Cararra quarries in northern Italy. The history of the shipwrecks can be seen in the museum in the loft of Tŷ Gwyn in Barmouth and Frank Cocksey's pierhead fishermen's sculpture was made from the shipwrecked marble.

Before the Lifeboat Institute was established in 1824, the inhabitants of Barmouth already provided their own life-saving service at sea. A boat was kept in the cellar of Pen y Cei, the building in which the Maritime Museum and the harbourmaster's office are now situated. Previously, the brave crews would have nothing except oars and sails to assist them in saving sailors from the jaws of the storms. The RNLI station was opened in Barmouth in 1828 but motorboats were not used by the service until 1904. Rowing boats ceased to be used in 1948.

Fast, inshore rescue craft came into operation in the Lifeboat station in Barmouth in 1967. By then, the demands on the service were changing in line with the changing nature of maritime traffic. Now, instead of ocean going ships running into trouble in storms, it was visitors in small boats and inexperienced swimmers who were responsible for most of the emergency callouts. Having a high-speed craft which was easily launched near the beach was essential. This boat is located near the old bathhouse and it can be on its way with a crew of three within a few seconds. It can forge its way through a heavy swell and reach places which would be impossible for a larger lifeboat. Over the years the lifeboat has rescued dozens of individuals in distress and up to the year 2000, the total number of people saved by the lifeboat at Barmouth was 522, and a number of crew members have received medals in recognition of their exceptional courage in carrying out their voluntary work at sea.

Barmouth harbour from Fairbourne

Llanfair Slates

There is plenty of high quality Cambrian slate under the Rhinogydd in north-west Meirionnydd, but the rock in this area is inaccessible and difficult to work. The only place where it could be reached easily was at Llanfair near Harlech which, for a while, became the site of a major quarrying community. Before the days of the railway, Llanfair slates were transported to Pensarn and exported on ships from there.

Llanfair was a quarry which used the underground method of accessing the slate – huge cathedral-like caverns were opened up in the heart of the mountain from the 1860s onwards. A series of layers of good quality slate were worked which descended in five galleries below the surface. This was the only quarry in the area and the history of its production was stormy; it is possible that it was the cost of its method of operation which was responsible for this. The quarry was closed after a few years but re-opened at the beginning of the twentieth century. The First World War put an end to its activity for a while, then it became a site for crushing rocks for a powder which was used in the production of tiles, employing twenty men. Explosives were stored in the safety of the caverns during the Second World War.

There are still a few quayside buildings to be seen at Pensarn, the relics of the export trade which was conducted from there at one time. After the Cambrian Railway reached the area, slates were transported by train.

The caverns were opened as a visitor attraction in the 1960s. With the aid of electricity and powerful lighting, it is possible for visitors today to see the wonder of these underground caves which were never seen by the quarrymen themselves who were hewing the rock by candlelight over a hundred years ago. It was in these caverns that some of the scenes from *First Knight* were filmed. A few of the original buildings still remain and many of the adits have been made safe and are open to the public, where old tools and wagons are on display. There is also a café and a shop selling slate crafts.

The crags of the Rhinogydd are renowned for their mineral wealth – to the south-east, between the peaks and the town of Dolgellau, lie the most important gold mines on the island of Britain. Between Barmouth and Bontddu in the south and Harlech and Trawsfynydd in the north, 44,000 tonnes of manganese were extracted from the western slopes of the Rhinogydd: there were 17 mines in all in the period between 1892-1928. Remains of buildings are still to be seen by the roadside along Afon Artro valley – Coed and Dôl Bebin – but most of them are located in very remote places.

Slate caverns open to the public at Llanfair

Dolgellau

Dolgellau, in the shadow of Cader Idris and lying on Afon Wnion, a tributary of Afon Mawddach, has more listed buildings than any other town in Wales – more than 200 of them. Some of the most elegant date back to Dolgellau's time as a regional centre for the Welsh woollen industry. It is traditionally the county town of the historic county of Meirionnydd, which lost its administrative status when Gwynedd was created in 1974. Today, it has revived its market town status after being freed of its traffic problems when the bypass was built – it is crafted from the character of the local stone and is a centre for local produce and culture. Every July it becomes a Welsh, Celtic and world folk hive of activity when the Sesiwn Fawr festival is held on its streets and in its pubs.

Historically, the town's most important industry was wool. However through the 18th and 19th centuries the town experienced a boom in the tanning industry that was followed by a gold rush. Today, Dolgellau's economy relies mainly on tourism although agriculture continues to play a significant role, and as such a local farmers' market is held in the town on the third Sunday of every month, and each Friday, the town holds a *diwrnod sêl* or market day.

Cymer abbey in nearby Llanelltyd, founded in 1198, was the most important religious centre locally. It is associated with many of the Welsh princes of Gwynedd. During the 12th century a church was built for the inhabitants of the town. This building was later demolished and replaced by the current church built in 1716. It seems that from the mid 12th century, Dolgellau gained in importance, and as such was mentioned in the Survey of Meirioneth ordered by Edward I. Later in 1404, during Owain Glyndŵr's national uprising, Dolgellau became the location of a council of Welsh leaders, led by Glyndŵr himself.

The town was the centre of a minor gold rush in the 19th century. At one time

1. *Cymer abbey*
2. *Tŷ Siamas folk centre at Dolgellau*

LLWYBR MAWDDACH

the local gold mines employed over 500 workers. Clogau St David's mine in Bontddu and Gwynfynydd mine in Ganllwyd have supplied gold for many famous couples.

Today, Dolgellau welcomes many thousands of visitors annually. Many come from across the Atlantic to trace their ancestry, others to walk and enjoy the stunning scenery and taste the local culture. It is a haven for walkers and climbers who enjoy the challenges of the nearby mountain ranges including the famous Cader Idris.

Penmaenpool

Penmaenpool (*Llynpenmaen*) is a hamlet on the south side of the estuary of Afon Mawddach near Dolgellau. A Grade II listed toll bridge provides access across the estuary for light vehicles under 1.5 tonnes.

The wooden toll bridge was built in 1879 to replace a ferry crossing and links the A493 running along the south bank of the Mawddach to the A496 running along the north. It is Cadw-registered and was Grade II listed in 1990. Around 200 crossings are made each day.

Fifteen people, including four children, were drowned on 22 July 1966 when the ferry *Prince of Wales* hit the toll bridge. The ferry had been taking 39 people on a pleasure trip from Barmouth to the hotel in the village. Though 27 lives were saved, nobody was officially recognised for bravery. A memorial was held by the signal box on the 50th anniversary of the disaster in 2016, and a plaque was unveiled commemorating the victims.

The George III Inn was originally two buildings: a ship chandler serving the boatbuilding industry, and a pub. It dates from approximately 1650. Gerard Manley Hopkins reputedly wrote the poem entitled 'Penmaen Pool' in the visitor's book.

Penmaenpool railway station was on the Aberystwyth and Welsh Coast Railway. It opened on 3 July 1865, and closed to goods on 4 May 1964 and passengers on 18 January 1965. The route is now part of the Mawddach Trail and is popular with walkers and cyclists.

1. Penmaenpool toll bridge; 2. Mawddach Trail; 3. George III Inn at Penmaenpool.

Aberdyfi and Tywyn

Between Dysynni and Dyfi

The beauty of the Meirionnydd estuaries cannot fail to move you. Most of these rivers flow from the east to meet the waters of Bae Ceredigion in the west, where they create a rich scenic tapestry of beach and dune, against a backdrop of high mountain ridges and clear waters. Two of these rivers are Dysynni and Dyfi and between them lies the area of Aberdyfi and Tywyn – a hidden gem often overlooked.

The seas here have their quota of legends concerning saints and pirates, as well as fishermen's yarns still told to this day. In the mountains there are lush green river valleys and remote cwms accessible on foot, by rail or on two or four wheels.

On the shoreline and hills, traces of human habitation – whether it be an ancient fort, an old church, a ruined castle or an old boat – are a constant reminder that this area is a treasure trove of stories worth telling.

Mountain and Lake

The hills around Tywyn and the Dyfi estuary rise gradually to the foot of the highest mountain, Cader Idris, 878m in height. Cader Idris was once a volcano and when active was responsible for shaping the surrounding valleys.

Craig y Deryn, Dysynni

According to legend, Idris was a giant and his *cader* (chair) was the mountain. It is hardly surprising that Idris enjoyed relaxing in this particular location, with the views from the summit of Cader Idris being particularly spectacular – better than those from the summit of *Yr Wyddfa* (Snowdon) according to many hill walkers.

Reaching its summit (Pen y Gader) in time to watch the sunset over Bae Ceredigion is a tradition among mountaineers. Another tradition is to spend the night on the mountain to watch the sun rise in the east in the morning – but you have to take care in respect of the latter. There is an old belief associated with the mountain that whoever sleeps there will either die or wake up insane or a poet.

The ridges of Cader Idris

Maen Cadfan (Cadfan's stone)

One of the most important historical relics in Wales is to be seen in the church at Tywyn – Maen Cadfan. Inscribed on the stone is, according to the experts, the oldest written example of the Welsh language. It consists of a carved stone pillar, oblong in shape, with words inscribed on all sides.

Maen Cadfan was carved around the year 750 AD. Along with the epitaphs on the stone are inscribed the words CUN BEN CELEN – TRICET NITANAM ('Cun, wife of Celen – the wound remains). Even today, it is possible to see the relationship between the contemporary Welsh we use and the older form.

Those named are: Celen; also Cun, the wife of Celen; Tengrui, the lawful wife of Adgan and the remains of 'three others' and 'four others' are also recorded on the stone. This is proof that prominent local families used Welsh rather than Latin even on their memorial stones. It supports all other evidence that Welsh is one of Europe's oldest literary languages.

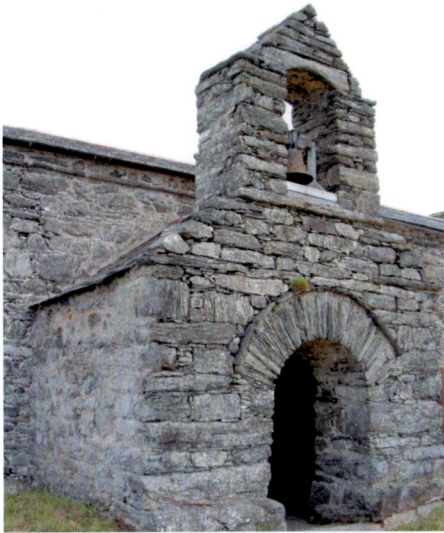

Other Old Churches:

Llangelynnin

This church is dedicated to Celynnin, a Welsh saint who was the son of Helig of Llys Helig. The ancient church is a marvellous building and it was recently restored, with due respect being paid to all its intrinsic features, the unadorned slate floor, the wooden benches and its air of simplicity. It is likely that the original building dates from 12th-13th century and was restored during the 15th century. Just outside the main doorway there is a flat stone inscribed with the initials AW – according to local tradition, this was the grave of the first Romany to be buried in Wales.

Llanegryn

The fine oak rood screen at Llanegryn church dates from the 14th century and separates the nave from the chancel. The roods and carvings have been lost, but the original carved panels are still intact in all their complex beauty. It is a national treasure and one of the few surviving original screens to be found anywhere in Wales.

Llanfihangel-y-pennant

In the far reaches of Dyffryn Dysynni, stands the church of Llanfihangel, nestling at the foot of the lower slopes of Cader Idris. The circular churchyard signifies the ancient nature of this devotional site. The present church dates from the 12th century and like many medieval churches, it has been dedicated to Mihangel (Michael). There is a leper's window on the north side. Because of the nature of that disease, the lepers were not allowed into the church itself, but they were allowed to follow the service from outside through the window provided.

Eglwys Fair (St Mary's) Tal-y-llyn

This small church stands on a hillock at the lower end of Llyn Myngul. The barrel-sided ceiling has been constructed from planks above the altar and is covered with striking paintings from the 14th century. Behind and above the door, there is an *englyn* (4-line strict metre stanza) which welcomes all those who come there in the right spirit.

Aberdyfi –
the meeting place of princes

Afon Dyfi is one of Wales' natural boundaries with three mediaeval regions conjoining on its banks – Gwynedd, Powys and Deheubarth. Many important declarations were made on the banks of the Dyfi which served as a convenient meeting place to discuss issues of national importance.

The village of Aberdyfi originally grew around a number of taverns and rest houses associated with the ferry that would cross the estuary in the Middle Ages. The Romans discovered copper in the hills nearby and they built a fort to control the ford in Pennal a little further upstream.

In the 6th century, Maelgwn Gwynedd summoned all the princes throughout Wales together on the south beach at the mouth of Afon Dyfi (near Ynys-las today). His intention was to settle who should become high-king, and a competition was organised to test their courage. Each prince brought his throne along with him and, at low tide, placed it on the beach – which is still called Traeth Maelgwn. As the tide turned, it was agreed that the last one to leave his throne and flee the rising waters would be the high-king of Wales. The regional kings had brought along very grand thrones which were richly adorned with precious metals and stones so that they could make an impression – all of them except Maelgwn. He sat on a seat made of goose feathers held together with wax which floated gently while all the other competitors wallowed in the rising tide. Maelgwn won easily, and henceforth it was to Gwynedd that the rest of Wales looked for leadership to preserve its independence.

In 1140 the clerics of Wales convened in Aberdyfi and at this meeting protested against Canterbury's interference in Welsh ecclesiastical affairs. They were adamant that they had an independent church, much older than the institution in England.

In the 13th century, Llywelyn Fawr of Gwynedd became a past master at resisting the Normans who were intent on usurping and governing Wales as they pleased. They did not succeed, however, and after a lifetime of successful resistance, Llywelyn called the leaders of Wales together on the banks of Afon Dyfi,

Aberdyfi, looking upriver from the quay

where, in 1216, the Treaty of Aberdyfi was drawn up confirming all Llywelyn's gains and proclaiming him as the overlord of Wales.

Several centuries later, Aberdyfi saw magnificent ships from France, Spain and Scotland sailing in on the tide and heading up Afon Dyfi as far as Derwen-las. From there, their passengers – ambassadors and representatives of their monarchs – travelled to Machynlleth for the first meeting of the senedd of Wales. The year was 1404, and Owain Glyndŵr, the father of modern Wales, had set the whole of Wales alight and was waging a war of independence. Representatives were summoned to the town on the banks of Afon Dyfi where Owain was proclaimed prince.

Over the centuries, meetings on the banks of Afon Dyfi have played a critical part in the development of modern Wales.

Aberdyfi and Traeth Maelgwn (to the right)

Castell y Bere

Although the Normans succeeded in making a few incursions into Wales, the Welsh stood firm and defeated them at the battle of Coed Yspwys in 1094, driving them out of Gwynedd and the west. The Welsh were not conquered as the English had been. Hardly any Normans had ventured into Meirionnydd for two centuries.

Llywelyn Fawr exercised a strong influence in this area in the 13th century. He was a great advocate of commerce and established a small town and market at Tywyn. Around 1221, he built a castle, originally of wood, and later of stone, at Castell y Bere on a rocky crest above Afon Dysynni. He employed 200 stone masons to undertake the work and paid them a penny a day. The elongated D-shaped towers, which were less likely to collapse if they were undermined during an attack or siege than square (English) towers, were a feature of Welsh castle-building at that time.

Castell y Bere stands today in a beautiful and romantic setting, a symbol of Welsh pride. The Welsh preferred to utilise the rugged independence of the mountains in the defence of their country, and Castell y Bere is a classic example of this.

Castell y Bere was a military centre for Llywelyn Fawr and Llywelyn ap Gruffudd – his grandson – who continued his campaign for independence during the latter half of the 13th century. With the exception of Caernarfon and Conwy, this is the largest castle in northern Wales and although its impressive walls have long since lain in ruin, their strength and design remain a source of admiration.

Llywelyn ap Gruffudd was killed in 1282. His brother Dafydd, continued the fight with limited resources. This castle was the last stronghold to fall into Norman hands after being besieged by an army of 3,000 in 1284. Edward I stayed there during November of that year, ordering the expansion of the walls and the establishment of a borough nearby. His ambitions to colonise the area came to an abrupt end. When the Welsh rose up in revolt in 1294 and destroyed the castle, the English abandoned both fortress and colony.

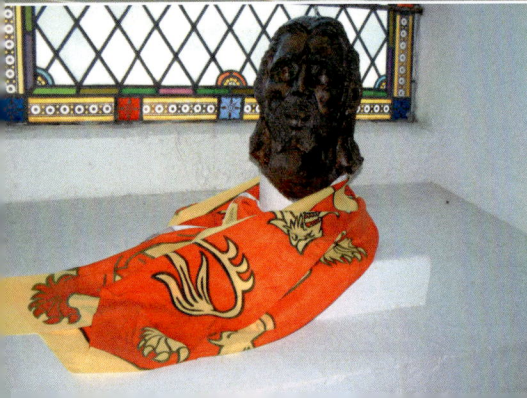

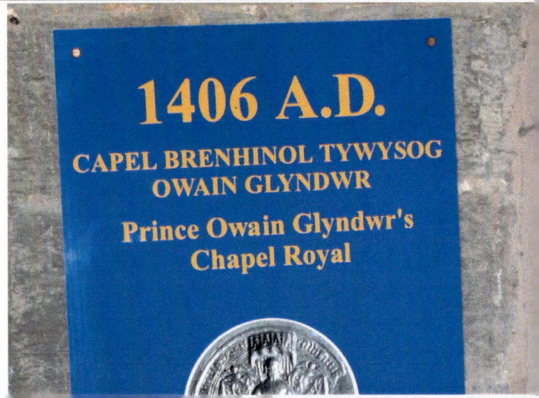

1406 A.D.

CAPEL BRENHINOL TYWYSOG
OWAIN GLYNDWR

Prince Owain Glyndwr's
Chapel Royal

Pennal

There is a strong sense of independence to be felt at the church in Pennal, which was established in the 6th century by Sant Tannwg and Sant Eithrias, both Celtic missionaries from Brittany. This church served several of the Welsh princes. During Lent 1406, Owain Glyndŵr held his final senedd in the village. Llythyr Pennal (*the Pennal letter*) is one of the most important documents in Welsh history, and is today kept in a Parisian archive. Owain Glyndŵr probably signed it in Pennal church on 31 March 1406 and sent it to Charles VI, king of France. A facsimile copy is displayed in the church.

In part of the letter, Glyndŵr outlines his programme and vision for the future of Wales – and it has been the basis for the political programme for Wales for centuries. By the end of the 20th century, implementation of each and every one of its main aims had been set in motion. Llythyr Pennal in itself provides a sufficient reason for Owain Glyndŵr to be called the father of modern Wales.

As part of the celebrations of the 600th anniversary of Glyndŵr's rebellion in 2000, Llythyr Pennal was returned temporarily from the Archives Nationales in Paris to form part of a popular exhibition at *Llyfrgell Genedlaethol Cymru* (National Library of Wales) in Aberystwyth.

Here in Pennal church, there is an interpretation centre which includes a number of interesting historical items and works of art.

Glyndŵr's power base was Harlech castle and when the tides of war turned against him, he lost possession of the castle. His family were taken to the Tower of London and many of his men were killed. However, he did not give up the struggle – he went underground and continued to fight a guerrilla campaign. There is a cave which bears his name in cliffs near the mouth of Afon Dysynni. Many stories grew up about his incredible ability to strike at the enemy and escape unscathed. He was transformed from being an historical hero to becoming a mythical figure. His death went unannounced and no one knows where he is buried. It was the longest revolt in the history of what was later called the British Empire.

The Tal-y-llyn
Narrow Gauge Railway

Whilst travelling in one of its carriages through the quiet Meirionnydd countryside, or enjoying the atmosphere of the Victorian week or the Santa Claus express at Christmas, it is easy to forget that this was at one time essentially an industrial railway line. When Bryneglwys quarry was developed, at a height of 300m above sea level, in 1864, it was on the wrong side of the mountain to take advantage of the Dyfi tramway which linked Corris and Machynlleth with the harbour at Derwen-las. It was a laborious task transporting the slates on the back of mules and sledges along the rough tracks from Pennal and on to Aberdyfi. When the quarry was enlarged, a tramway was developed from Bryneglwys down to Nant Gwernol to Abergynolwyn and then a narrow gauge line running through Dôl-goch, Brynglas and Rhydyronnen to the slate quay in Tywyn. The only substantial construction work involved was the building of an impressive three-arched viaduct at Dôl-goch.

The main coast line from Aberdyfi to Llwyngwril had been opened since 1863,

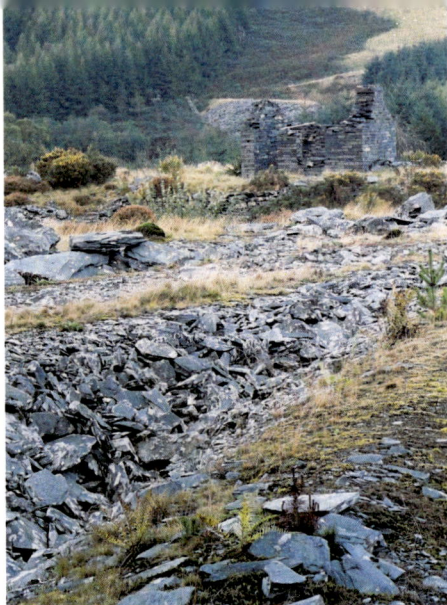

Bryneglwys slate quarry

and thus Tywyn became a convenient depot for slate, to be reloaded onto main line trains and despatched to the English Midlands or on to sailing ships from Aberdyfi. From the outset, the Tal-y-llyn railway was designed to carry passengers as well as slates and this was the first narrow gauge railway in the world designed entirely for steam locomotives. To this day, only steam locomotives are

used to pull the carriages.

When the quarry closed in 1947, the owner, Sir Henry Haydn Jones, the Member of Parliament for Meirionnydd who lived in Tywyn, kept the line open for the community. This cost him £5 a week until his death in 1950. The Tal-y-llyn Railway Preservation Society was formed and in February 1951, the railway was transferred into its care. This was the first

Tal-y-llyn railway

railway in the world to be saved and restored for the tourist industry.

The railway was extended from Abergynolwyn to Nant Gwernol during the 1970s. The appeal of the line and its little trains is now legendary. Some 30,000 passengers travel on it annually, enjoying the scenery, its gentle rhythms, getting a taste of a past age and using it as public transport to travel from one delightful station to the next.

At Cei Tywyn station, you can also visit the narrow gauge museum, which houses the best collection in the island of Britain of artefacts relating to narrow gauge railways. There are over 90 railways represented in the museum – which includes locomotives, trucks, signals, posters, lamps, tickets, signs, name plates, rails and all sorts of other treasures to excite historical railway enthusiasts. The purpose of the narrow gauge railway, of course, was to offer a cheaper form of transport, which was easier to build in rural areas where the terrain was difficult for a standard gauge line. It is not surprising therefore that Wales is world-famous for its tradition of 'great little trains'.

The station and museum at Tywyn

Aberdyfi Harbour

Lead, silver, copper and zinc were all mined in the surrounding hills, and the harbour became an obvious outlet for exporting ore. Another export was oak for the shipbuilding industry. In 1827, a new road was cut along the coast from Tywyn to Aberdyfi and from there to Pennal and Machynlleth, and this was followed by the Cambrian Coast Railway in 1863.

Today, as you walk along the shore at Aberdyfi, it is difficult to imagine the hive of activity here when the harbour was in its heyday. Slates from Bryneglwys quarry would be brought by the little train to the quay at Aberdyfi built by the Cambrian Company in 1882, where previously sea spray had lashed fishermen's cottages. The site of the modern-day car park was covered by a network of rails carrying trucks for loading and unloading.

Another stretch of railway was opened up to Machynlleth in 1867 and when this linked up with the Aberdyfi line, slates from the quarries at Corris and Aberllefenni, together with lead from Dylife, were brought to the harbour at the mouth of Afon Dyfi. For a while there was every possibility that Aberdyfi would develop as a port for Ireland. That never transpired, but steamers used to plough back and forth to Waterford. As recently as 1900, over 200 ships called at Aberdyfi, to unload coal and lime and collect cargos of slate and lead.

Shipbuilding was another important industry which developed in conjunction with the harbour. A number of shipyards were built along the shore at Aberdyfi – there were seven yards at Penhelig alone. Over one hundred oak ships were built there using wood from the Dyfi forest. Local oak was particularly suitable for making masts. It is strange to think that some of these ships rounded the Horn to return with guano from Chile and Peru.

Saving lives at sea was an important concern at the little port. The first lifeboat arrived in 1837 and a new shed was erected to house it at Penhelig in 1884, the lifeboat remaining in operation until 1931. Nowadays a fast inshore rescue craft operates from the village.

With the decline in the old industries, the harbour was neglected and the winter storms left their scars. In 1965, the quay came into the care of the town council and seven years later action was taken to

protect the harbour by means of an outer wall of steel around the old wooden frame. The old railway tracks were taken up and the warehouses demolished, a maritime garden, promenade and car parks being developed in their place. The words of the song, 'Clychau Aberdyfi' are reflected in the logo (a black bell on a white sail) of the Dyfi Sailing Club formed in 1949.

Aberdyfi from Ynys-las (left); old boat posts at Aberdyfi harbour

The Market Town of Machynlleth

Wales' Central Metropolis

Machynlleth is the market town of the Dyfi valley – a relaxed and homely sort of place situated at the point where the steep-sided valley terrain gives way to open countryside and the river flows to meet the rising tides. The shops, galleries and streets are colourful and attractive and are particularly lively on a Wednesday, market day.

Machynlleth has a railway station which provides a link with other nearby towns, such as Aberystwyth (29km), *Drenewydd* (Newtown) (49km), Tywyn (20km) and Porthmadog (67km). Several roads meet here and neither Dolgellau (26km) nor Llanidloes (32km) are too far away by car. In fact, it doesn't really matter which way you travel through Wales – from south to north, from east to west, or diagonally – Machynlleth and this area will probably be on your route.

The town has also enjoyed a central role in the history and politics of Wales. It was here that Owain Glyndŵr held his first national senedd.

To this day, Machynlleth is a good example of a town which has adapted and survived. It has accepted new ideas and has moved on with confidence. Machynlleth's vision remains central.

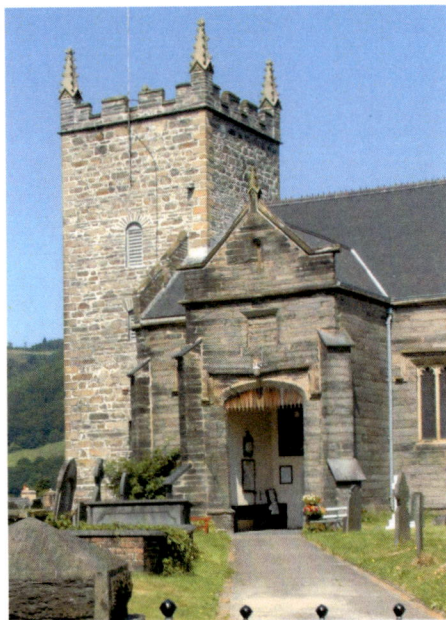

An old church and a modern bridge

The market and the wool trade

When Edward I established a network of castles and privileged colonial boroughs in their shadow, the Welsh were prevented from owning property or holding office or from having any rights within their walls. They were also prohibited from holding a market within ten miles of these new towns.

Machynlleth is typical of a Welsh town which developed far from the orbit of the castles and Norman coastal towns. It grew to serve an extensive rural hinterland in the surrounding valleys and mountains, where farmers could market their produce and craftsmen and small industries could establish themselves. A weekly market has been held since 1291 in Machynlleth and the old names of its broad streets, which form a letter 'T', suggest that it drew people from far and wide, with the Welsh opting to avoid Aberystwyth and its English garrison. Heol Gwŷr y Deheubarth (*the road of the men of the south*) was the old name given to present-day Heol Pentrerhedyn; Heol Gwŷr y Gogledd (*the north*) the name given to Heol Penrallt and Heol Gwŷr Cyfeiliog was the original name for Heol Maen-gwyn – representing the three main kingdoms of Wales.

The sheep and cattle drovers and tanners, wool-staplers and purveyors of traditional Welsh cloth would come from far and wide to do business at Machynlleth market. Livestock would be driven all the way from the English Midlands, Essex, Kent and Sussex. The expansion of London during the 16th and 17th centuries gave a boost to market towns such as Machynlleth in Wales.

The last traditional Welsh drovers were Dafydd Isaac and John George from Ceredigion. They both did business at Machynlleth market between 1911 and 1932, driving their sheep every week from the pens near Pont-ar-Ddyfi to *Aberhonddu* (Brecon).

The wool industry grew up in the farmsteads in the area – originally it was a cottage industry and the product would be carried on ponies to the markets at Oswestry and Shrewsbury. By the end of the 16th century, a number of weavers had established full-time workshops in the town, with the wool being supplied by sheep, which were kept on the hills or the nearby common ground. Cottages built by weavers in 1826 are to be seen on the right-

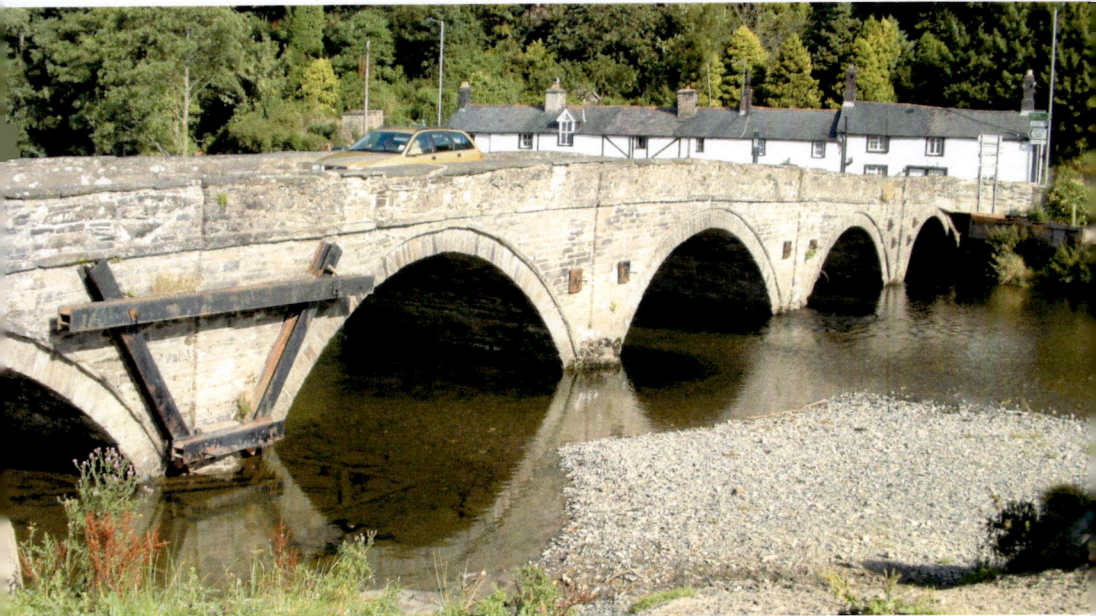

hand side as you look down Stryd Brickfield from Sgwâr y Garsiwn.

By the 19th century, the industry had been centralised in factories powered by water-wheels on the edge of town and in other villages in the area. There were a dozen wool manufacturers and five cloth manufacturers in the Machynlleth area by 1860. With the advent of the railway to Machynlleth in 1863, however, there was a gradual decline in this old industry as the huge woollen mills of Yorkshire began to undercut the prices. Before long, all fleeces were being taken from the area to Yorkshire, where the entire manufacturing process would take place.

The Glyndŵr Years

Machynlleth's special place in Welsh history is inexorably linked with the father of contemporary Wales, Owain Glyndŵr. Racist legislation which oppressed the Welsh could only be enacted and implemented for so long, before the tension between the Norman lords and boroughs in Wales and the Welsh people and their natural leaders exploded in open rebellion.

This eventually happened in 1400. The flame was initially ignited in northern Powys when Owain Glyndŵr lead a raid against the tyrannical usurper of the land, Lord Grey of Rhuthun. The town was razed to the ground on market day. It rapidly became a national uprising and the Welsh flocked from every part of the country to support Glyndŵr.

Wales was ablaze. Glyndŵr was proclaimed *Tywysog Cymru* (Prince of Wales) by his followers and no English borough or castle was safe from attack in the long struggle which ensued.

Early in the summer of 1401, Owain turned south with his army. He crossed Afon Dyfi and raised his standard – a golden dragon on a white background – on

The Glyndŵr memorial stone in the park

the summit of Pumlumon. Another of Glyndŵr's heraldic emblems was the black lion – the old coat of arms of the princes of Powys – and the emblem and name is still to be found on a number of inns and taverns to this day.

In the mountains of Pumlumon, to the south of Machynlleth, Owain experienced one of his first victories on the battlefield. Glyndŵr and his small force of some 500 men were gathered on the high ground above the banks of the Hyddgen river. An army of some 1,500 came up against them from their Norman enclaves in southern Pembrokeshire.

The enemy force encircled the Welsh encampment, but realising that the net was closing in on them, Owain led his men in a daring raid against the lowest arc of the circle and succeeded in breaking out. He used the terrain and the position of the sun to his advantage. He was an extremely accomplished strategist and military colleges still study his tactics He left hundreds of his adversaries lying dead on the slopes of Hyddgen. Two white stones known as Cerrig Cyfamod Owain, (*Owain's covenant stones*) can be seen at the site to this day and the secondary

school at Machynlleth is called Bro Hyddgen. The artist, Murray Urquhart, has painted an impressive picture of the battle of Hyddgen on the ceiling of the *senedd-dy* (parliament building) at Machynlleth.

The summer of 1404 was probably the greatest in the history of Machynlleth – and, indeed, has enormous significance in the history of Wales. By the time of the solstice in June of that year, Owain Glyndŵr was at the height of his career and was beginning to lay the foundations of a new political order for the future of his country. His dream of an independent Wales, standing shoulder to shoulder with other European nations, was about to be realised.

The English castles of Harlech and Aberystwyth had fallen into his hands and his armies had obliterated several other towns which had grown up in the shadow of the invaders' fortresses. He won important battles, sending fear through the ranks of his opponents. Careful diplomacy meant that several of his erstwhile enemies became his allies and he was corresponding with, and sending ambassadors to, the kings of Scotland, Ireland, Spain and France.

In 1399, Prince Hal, the son of Henry IV of England, had been proclaimed 'Prince of Wales' in London – as was the case with the firstborn sons of English monarchs since the time of Edward I. This incensed the Welsh even further, having already suffered a great deal at the hands of the English invaders. Owain was proclaimed Prince of Wales by his followers in September 1400. In the summer of 1404, he summoned four representatives from every commote in Wales to meet at Machynlleth, in order to convene a Welsh senedd which would confirm Owain as Prince of Wales.

The assembled representatives met in the open air where Owain Glyndŵr's senedd-dy now stands in Heol Maengwyn, and it was there that Owain was proclaimed and crowned as Prince of his country in the presence of representatives from Scotland, France and Spain. It is believed that the senedd-dy was built on its present site a few years later to commemorate the colourful ceremony which had been celebrated there with such passion and enthusiasm under Owain's standard. It is still a popular interpretive centre.

The Parliament House museum

The Centre for Alternative Technology

In October 1973, Gerard Morgan-Grenville stumbled across the disused workings of Llwyngwern quarry, some two miles off the main road from Machynlleth to Corris. The quarry had closed in 1951, the modern age having no further use for it.

However, Gerard was not convinced that our greedy technological age, with its all-consuming appetite for resources and its indifference to the ability of our planet to continue to fulfill such an exhausting demand, was, in essence, a good thing. He conceived the idea of creating a centre in Llwyngwern quarry which would pioneer and popularise the principle of Alternative Technology. Many volunteers offered their help and over the years, the credibility of the Centre grew and has been given ever-increasing publicity.

Thirty years on, the Centre for Alternative Technology is one of central Wales' leading visitor attractions and enjoys worldwide recognition for the work which is undertaken there. Originally, there had been no intention to open the Centre to the public. Ostensibly the idea was to create an experimental and self-sufficient community. However, with the growth in green politics and the realisation by ordinary people that principles such as sustainability and conservation are crucial to the survival of life on the planet, public curiosity meant it was inevitable that the experiment would become a visitor attraction.

The Centre had to be adapted and popularised. By the end of the 1980s, the site entrance had become a problem. Funds were raised to buy a funicular railway to negotiate the steep slope from the car park to the Centre itself. This railway is powered by water pressure and gravity rather than electricity or a combustion engine. A tank underneath one carriage is filled with water from the Centre's reservoir at the top of the slope. The weight of that carriage as it descends then brings up the other one full of passengers. After the descending carriage has reached the bottom of the incline, the water is discharged from the tank and the process is repeated. This ingenious means of arriving at the Centre has become an attraction in itself!

The Centre is constantly being extended. Its aim is to inspire people to

search for alternative ways of living, and this is achieved through various exhibitions, organic gardens, green architecture, a restaurant offering delicious and healthy food, a large shop and intriguing footpaths. For the children, there is plenty of fun to be had trying out the various wind, solar and water energy apparatus, as well as an adventure park, farm animals and an underground journey in the company of Megan y Twrch Daear (*twrch daear*: mole).

There is a special discount for families – and also for those who use bikes or public transport to get there. In the town of Machynlleth there is another branch of the Centre – a café and a whole food shop called Siop y Chwarel (*the quarry shop*) in Heol Maen-gwyn. Also, on the edge of the town, Parc Eco Dyfi focuses on eco-technology. It is not surprising that the town is now known as the 'alternative capital of Wales'.

Aberystwyth

The town from Pendinas to Pen-glais

Geographically, only two miles separate Pendinas and Rhiw Pen-glais, two peaks that confront each other above the low-lying town of Aberystwyth. On Pendinas, with its concentric fortified walls, dwelt the Bronze Age and Iron Age people. Many of their primitive weapons have been discovered in the vicinity. On Pen-glais, on the Aberystwyth University campus, a robotic arm destined for the surface of Mars was fashioned by scientists.

The visible history of Aberystwyth should begin on Pendinas, the hill fort where people have kept a close watch on the sea and the land for over ten centuries. The monument that tops the hill is a more recent addition – a folly built by a local landowner in admiration of the Duke of Wellington in 1852. The circular tower is, apparently, a symbol of a cannon.

Weapons were important to this locality at a far earlier age. Below the hill on the flatland of Tan-y-bwlch, an arms factory existed during the New Stone Age. Here, simple stone weapons and implements were fashioned by nomadic tribes – hunters and fishermen who would wander in search of sustenance. The flintstones left behind by glacial movements during the Stone Age were perfect raw materials.

During the Iron Age, the hilltop became a fortified stronghold of earthen and stone banks, deep ditches and sturdy portals, an impregnable shelter for the Celts and their animals. This way of life brought about the custom of the seasonal moving of animals from lowland to highland in early summer and back again before the onset of winter. Evidence exists there of the cultivation of corn by those Celts that were the forefathers of the Welsh.

Two views of Aberystwyth

CANTRE'R GWAELOD

The Drowned Lands

The legend of Cantre'r Gwaelod (*the lowland hundred*) further north along the coast may well be based on fact. At a settlement where earthen banks kept out the waters of Bae Ceredigion, the keeper of the flood-gate was Seithennyn, and one night, having imbibed too much on mead he forgot to close the sluice. The waters flooded the settlement. To this day, old tree stumps are seen at low tide along the beach between Ynys-las and Aberdyfi, suggesting that this was once dry land.

Ceredigion Castles

In the north of Ceredigion, following Hugh, son of Lord Roger Montgomery's incursion from his stronghold in the Welsh Marches, castles began to be built. The early ones were earthen mounds and two were built to the north of Aberystwyth, Gwallter castle in Llanfihangel Genau'r Glyn and Ystradpeithyll castle near Capel Dewi. Goginan castle to the east followed and immediately south of Aberystwyth, Tanycastell was built. Most castles, or Norman edifices with the exception of Tomen Las on the Dyfi estuary and Penrhos Fort above Llanrhystud, were built by the Welsh.

Much is known of Tanycastell, built on the south bank of the Ystwyth near Tan-y-bwlch. This was the original Aberystwyth castle built by Cadwgan ap Bleddyn, who ruled the whole of Ceredigion during the early part of the 12th century. His son, Owain, was rather impetuous. In 1109 he led an attack on Pembroke castle where he kidnapped Nest, wife of the Constable. This provoked an attack on Ceredigion by Gilbert de Clare and his men and Owain and his father had to flee. Their land was given to Gilbert Fitzgerald who built

Welsh princes graves at Ystrad Fflur

Tanycastell. The castle regularly changed hands during skirmishes between the Welsh and the Normans and, as often as not, between the Welsh themselves.

It was nearby that the first ever battle to be described in detail took place. This was the Battle of Antaron at the beginning of the 12th century between the Normans and Gruffudd ap Rhys. Antaron Avenue between Penparcau and Rhydyfelin keeps the name alive.

The prime figure to emerge during the 12th century was Rhys ap Gruffudd, yr Arglwydd Rhys (*arglwydd*: lord). By 1172 he was acknowledged as leader of southern Wales. It was during his reign that Gerald the Welshman visited north Ceredigion during his attempt to raise an army to fight in the Crusades. His account of his visit tells of the beavers he had seen in the Dyfi, the purity of the Welsh language and the despicable way he was treated by the clerics at Llanbadarn.

Rhys died in 1197 when he was 65 years old having ruled Ceredigion for 30 years. His death led to the decimation of his kingdom by his sons. Then, two years following the death of Llywelyn ap Gruffudd in 1284, the Statute of Rhuddlan was made law thus allowing the King of England ownership of large areas of Wales. As a result, the area of Ceredigion between the Aeron and the Dyfi was ruled by Aberystwyth castle.

Laureate of Love and Nature

To the north of Aberystwyth near Penrhyn-coch, in the parish of Llanbadarn Fawr, only a few stones remain of Bro Gynin, home of Wales' greatest poet, Dafydd ap Gwilym.

The facts regarding Dafydd's life are few but it is acknowledged that he was at his greatest as a poet around 1350. He may have received his early education at *Ystrad Fflur* (Strata Florida abbey) and it is there that he is said to be buried. The name of the area around Bro Gynin is Tirymynach or Tir-y-myneich, *mynach* being monk. This area between two parishes used to belong to Ystrad Fflur.

Dafydd revolutionised the poetry of his day injecting fresh blood into his language and metre and introducing a new vigour to the art of the poet. He succeeded in uniting the old tradition with that of a vibrant expression of nature and daring love poems. His greatest contribution was in dragging Welsh poetry into the mainstream of European verse.

In his love poems, Dafydd sang of his feelings for Dyddgu and Morfudd, often unrequited love. The fact that Dyddgu was already married was no help. But Dafydd knew that a married mistress and cuckolded husband was a predominant and popular theme across the channel. He would often sing of his failures, and his song to the Ladies of Llanbadarn is a classic where he curses the girls for refusing his advances. Llanbadarn is a constant theme. In one poem, the flooded Dyfi prevents him from crossing to his favourite woman in his favourite parish. Llanbadarn has recognised Dafydd's greatness with an exhibition at the church.

His nature poems sing of the thrush, the nightingale and the lark and a constant theme is the poet sending birds as messengers of love to his current girlfriend.

At one time, three farmsteads were referred to as Bro Gynin. The building reputed to be Dafydd's home was demolished in 1972. Today a modern bungalow stands there. The original house was a small mansion but during the Great War, half the building was demolished and the stones used to repair the road.

In 1977 a memorial plaque was unveiled at Bro Gynin. Another one can be seen at Ystrad Fflur where, according to tradition, his grave lies.

A troubadour image at Llanbadarn church

Dafydd ap Gwilym's grave

Sea, Sail and Steam

In 1566, the ports of Aberystwyth and Llanrhystud were being placed under the authority of Aberdyfi. A campaign was also launched to curtail the activities of pirates, who were particularly active at the time.

All this coincided with the proliferation of lead mines in the north of the county and the increase in the woollen and fishing industries. During 1702, a total of 1,700 baskets of fish were exported to Ireland. The inward trade included salt from France and wood and iron hoops from Ireland to form casks. Also from Ireland, kindling, cabbage and turnip seed, wax and candles, soap and cloth were exchanged for slates and fish.

Trade was established with Norway, Holland, Spain and Portugal. One cargo of note was a shipload of oranges and lemons for Lord Lisburne. Unfortunately the delicacies never made it to Trawscoed. The ship was beached at Llanrhystud and all the fruit was lost.

The furthest voyage from Bae Ceredigion was a load of herring bound for the Canary Islands in 1701. But just as important as international trade was the Welsh coastal trade with smaller ships carrying corn, herring, slates, lead as well as salmon, beer and honey, cloth, stockings and iron.

By the 18th century, local seafaring companies began to build their own ships. In Aberystwyth alone, 278 ships were built between 1780 and 1880. The largest was the 1,100 ton *Caroline Spooner* launched in 1887. Other ships of note built at Aberystwyth included the barque *Anne Jenkins* and the brig *Credo*, both of them ferrying emigrants to America.

By 1851, lead carried to Holywell and Flint was still the mainstay of the local shipping industry. Still important was the export of bark to Ireland as well as oak and pine posts to Liverpool and pit props to southern Wales.

Being an entrepôt, or a distributing centre, cargo such as coal, fish and oil as well as common goods would be sent on from Aberystwyth to Porthmadog, Barmouth and Aberdyfi. During the 18th century, fishing boats from the Isle of Man were a common sight in the bay. But by the end of the century, herring was so scarce and so costly that it had to be imported from the Isle of Man.

Markets, Fairs and Drovers

Aberystwyth and Llanbadarn Fawr's fairs were founded in 1277. Those that lived between the Aeron and the Dyfi rivers would flock there to buy or sell goods and stock. Originally, two fairs were held at Aberystwyth on a field near the castle. Centuries later with the coming of the train, Llanbadarn Fair moved to the town. Two horse fairs were also held annually at Aberystwyth.

In the 18th century the Corn Market was built behind what became the Talbot Hotel. Later, in 1832, a new Corn Market was built nearby. There, as well as grain, cheese, wool and all kinds of agricultural produce was sold.

Meat was sold at Llanbadarn until the 18th century. Then meat began to be sold in the open air near the old Neuadd y Dref (Town Hall) until a purpose-built meat market was opened on St James' Square. The building is still used as a general market. Fish, of course, would be widely sold at the Fish Market on the ground floor of the old Town Hall. In 1871 work was completed on a third Market Hall, John James', where W. H. Smith stands today.

In 1724, author and traveller Daniel Defoe noted that Ceredigion was breeding cattle for the whole of England. The connection between the farmers and the English towns and cities was the drovers. They would buy cattle locally and then herd them in centres like Lledrod or Llanfarian. Cattle in the north of the county would be shoed on Pen-y-bont field in Llanbadarn before being walked to Tregaron through to Abergwesyn and Herefordshire and on to Barnet and Watford fairs.

As the agricultural industry flourished, the need arose for a local bank. This led to the opening of Banc y Ddafad Ddu – The Black Sheep Bank – in Bridge Street in 1810, close to Banc y Llong – the Ship Bank – opened in 1762, probably the first ever bank to be opened in Wales.

By Rail to Aberystwyth

The Cambrian Railway reached Aberystwyth in 1864, having come as far as Borth two years previously. A special train marked the occasion with 23 coaches carrying 600 passengers from Shrewsbury and Welshpool. The Manchester and Milford Railway from Caerfyrddin in the south was extended to Pencader and then to Ystrad Fflur. It reached Aberystwyth in 1867. The line was later taken over by the Great Western Railway until 1964, when Lord Beeching's axe fell. His villainous act was ironically commemorated in Aberystwyth at the beginning of the 90s when the Railway Hotel's name was changed to Lord Beechings.

The old station today

'The Brighton of Wales'

When visitors first discovered Aberystwyth towards the end of the 18th century, the town had only three hotels of quality, the Talbot being the best, then the Gogerddan Arms, and thirdly The Old Black Lion.

The most popular bathing spot was between what is now the Bandstand and the Pier. By 1826, 21 bathing machines were available there.

Hotels then began to appreciate the attractions of entertainment such as dances and harpists. The marching local Militia offered some excitement and of special interest to visitors were the Methodist meetings where the worshippers tended to jump up and down.

When that well-known traveller Wigstead visited at the end of the 18th century he described the town as 'the Brighton of Wales'. A brief attempt had been made to turn the town into a spa. A chalybeate well was opened near Plas Crug in 1779. There is still a Chalybeate Street in the town. There is an apocryphal tale of a policeman who, having found a dead donkey lying there and having to record the fact in his notebook, found it easier to drag the animal to Mill Street rather than attempt to spell Chalybeate.

A theatre was a necessity, of course. The town had already attracted travelling players to the old Town Hall. The first theatre opened in 1813 in a storehouse near Pont Trefechan. Today it is a bar and is known as Rummers. In 1828 a second theatre was opened on the corner of North Parade and Thespian Street. It is said that Sarah Siddons once trod the boards there and it is a fact that Henry Irving visited the town.

Over the years, other entertainment centres of note were opened in the town. The Queen's at the end of the prom, the Coliseum, a theatre and cinema which is now the home of Amgueddfa Ceredigion (*amgueddfa*: museum), Cheethams Picture Palace where today stands the Pantyfedwen Trust offices, the Skating Rink in Portland Street and the Bath House in, of course, Bath Street. The Pier Pavilion built in 1896 became a centre of importance and included a cinema. The King's Hall was built on the site of the Old Waterloo Hotel. But the venue where the Rolling Stones appeared in the 60s is now made up of flats. The Little Theatre was

closed in 1958. The Commodore Cinema remains as does the Arts Centre on the University Campus on Pen-glais. Fortunately, Cwmni Arad Goch – a

Amgueddfa Ceredigion

community theatre company – has made its home in Aberystwyth.

The College by the Sea

Despite the fact that Aberystwyth dates back to 1277, it is still a young town. Among the 18,000 inhabitants, some 8,000 are school or college students.

Aberystwyth boasts the oldest University College in Wales, opened in October 1872 in the old Castle Hotel. The first Principal was the Rev. Thomas Charles Edwards. He and three members of staff catered for 26 students who lodged in the town paying between 15s and 16s a week for full board. In July 1885, fire caused damage of £20,000 to the college building and three people died fighting the blaze. The building was restored and the student population rose to 132.

Owain Glyndŵr's dream of a Welsh university was realised through the work of a handful of fervent Welsh people funded by farmers and miners and they had to wait until 1889 for the Treasury to grant it its Charter. It then found the wholehearted support of David Davies of Llandinam.

In 1884, women were allowed to study there for the first time and Avergeldie Hall was opened to accommodate them. Carpenter Hall followed in 1919.

The most controversial Principal in the history of the college was Goronwy Rees who resigned in 1957 after only four years at the helm. Then, under the leadership of Thomas Parry came the great expansion. The college spread to the new campus on Pen-glais and the student population rose to 1,500 and then to 2,000 by 1969. Soon afterwards, Pantycelyn Hall became a Welsh hall of residence.

It is also outward-looking, with strong links with the Celtic world and other European countries.

Exciting developments can be seen at the old university building at the sea front. The vision is to bring new life to Old College, a Grade 1 listed building and home of the first University College of Wales and to transform this iconic building into a major cultural and creative centre for Wales.

The House of Treasures

If your idea of a library is a dark, decaying building full of cobweb-covered books then you won't have visited the National Library of Wales recently.

After over a century since its founding in 1911, the library has witnessed some of the greatest changes in its history. Recently a shop, a new restaurant and two exhibition areas were opened together with a multi-purpose auditorium, The Drum, which has conference and film facilities.

The library now holds over 6 million books, 40,000 manuscripts, 4 million archives and 750,000 photographs as well as art collections, films, videos and sound recordings of every kind.

Aberystwyth had to battle long and hard for the right to secure the National Library. Cardiff also coveted this unique institution. Ultimately, after much squabbling, there came a truce – Aberystwyth would get the library and Cardiff the National Museum.

Today, the library shares its site with the Celtic Studies Centre which is administered by the University of Wales.

Aberystwyth was one of the first areas in Wales to adopt the Public Libraries and Museums Act of 1871. The public library was located in many buildings before settling in its present home, with the county archives, at Queen's Square.

Llyfrgell Genedlaethol Cymru

Great Little Trains of Aberystwyth

One of Aberystwyth's most popular assets is the Vale of Rheidol narrow gauge line running 12 miles from the town to *Pontarfynach* (Devil's Bridge) which offers natural attractions such as the Mynach Falls and the Devil's Cauldron as well as the famous three bridges that span the gorge immediately above each other.

The lowest of the three bridges is reputed to have been built by the devil. Legend tells of old Marged, whose cow, Malen, had wandered to the other side of the gorge. Marged and her dog, Smala, were suddenly accosted by a stranger who offered to build a bridge across the gorge with the proviso that he could possess the first living being to cross. Marged agreed and the stranger built the bridge before her very eyes. Marged then tossed a loaf of bread over the bridge. Smala ran to pick up the loaf and the stranger, realising he had been tricked, revealed a pair of horns and a tail. The bridge is still referred to today by some people as Pont y Gŵr Drwg (*gŵr drwg*: devil) but the name of the river is found in the Welsh place-name Pontarfynach.

The Vale of Rheidol Line was originally opened in 1902 to carry lead and timber from the uplands to the harbour. But gradually, as the mines closed, it became a tourist attraction.

The line was built narrower than what was normal for two reasons – one was financial the other practical. The hilly terrain along Dyffryn Rheidol posed quite a problem so the line meanders and is steep in places. But despite the fact that it is just less than two feet wide, the track carries engines weighing 25 tons and measuring eight feet across.

The original locomotives and carriages were built in Swindon by Great Western Railway between 1923 and 1938 and the line managed to overcome all kinds of problems both in ownership and in the uncertainty of its future. This was the last steam railway owned by British Rail when it was privatised in 1989.

Aberystwyth has a second train that is rather out of the ordinary. Climbing Constitution Hill, or Craiglais on the sea front is the Cliff Railway which at 778 feet long is the longest electric railway in Britain. The coaches, by Croydon Marks, were built aslant to negotiate the slope. It

DEVIL'S BRIDGE
(PONTARFYNACH)

Cambrian Coast 2

was opened in 1896 and was originally powered by water weight but since 1921 it was adapted to electric power with steel cables pulling the carriages along at an amazing four miles an hour up to the summit. There passengers can view the largest Camera Obscura in the world with its 14 inch lens offering a 360 degree view over 1,000 square miles of land and sea. The view is projected onto a screen in the viewing gallery below.

The building also houses a historical exhibition and craft shop and refreshments are provided in the nearby Summer Teahouse Rooms.

The Cliff Railway

Wildlife Reserves

The **Dyfi National Nature Reserve** is situated midway between Aberystwyth and Machynlleth. It includes the dunes of Ynys-las on the southern side of Dyfi estuary which are the largest dunes in Ceredigion. The estuary has vast areas of internationally important mudflats, sandbanks and saltmarsh that provide feeding and roosting areas for wetland birds. The Ynys-las Visitor Centre is the ideal place to start a visit. It has an exhibition about what to see at the reserve, and a shop selling hot and cold drinks, snacks, books and local produce.

Further upriver, the **RSPB reserve at Ynys-hir** offers a wide range of seasonal varieties. Flocks of wintering wigeon, lapwing and teal can be seen especially around high tides from the Saltings or Ynys Feurig hides. Spring is spectacular. Pied flycatchers and redstarts sing in the woods, and the woodland floor in late April and May is covered in a purple haze of bluebells. Quiet pools can give close views of otters and kingfishers. If you don't fancy a walk, the visitor centre bird feeders are alive with birds.

The **Dyfi Osprey Project** is based at Cors Dyfi Reserve, near Derwen-las, under the management of the Montgomeryshire Wildlife Trust. In 2011, for the first time in over 400 years, ospreys have been breeding in the Dyfi valley. From the facilities, visitors can view live streaming of the local ospreys' nest. A wetland walk has been constructed and a fine 360° Observatory. From the upper viewing level, 10 m (33 ft) above the bog below, the building provides a panoramic view, enhancing the visitor experience to the full range of flora and fauna on the reserve.

Bwlch Nant yr Arian Forest Visitor Centre is perched on a dramatic hilltop, straddling the boundary between the lowlands and uplands, and has commanding views of Bae Ceredigion and the Cambrian Mountains. It is well-known for its long-established tradition of daily feeding of red kites. There is also a skills park with a purpose-built track for mountain bikers to practice their technique and a waymarked trail for horse riders.

1. Observatory at Dyfi Osprey; 2. Ynys-las Centre; 3. Bwlch Nant yr Arian Centre

The Capital of the Welsh Language

If Cardiff is the capital of Wales, it can be reasonably argued that Aberystwyth is the capital of our native tongue, Welsh.

It was at Aberystwyth that Urdd Gobaith Cymru, Europe's largest youth movement was founded in 1922 with its headquarter at Llanbadarn Road. It was in that same building that the first Welsh medium primary school was opened in 1939. From seven pupils, taught by Miss Norah Isaac, and having moved to Lluest Gwilym on Waunfawr, it grew to 118 pupils and a staff of six by 1946. That year, with Hywel D. Roberts as headmaster, the pupils were integrated into the new Welsh School at Alexandra Road. Penweddig School then became one of the first Welsh Medium Comprehensives in Wales in 1973.

To the north in Penrhyn-coch the Farmers Union of Wales has its head office and Aberystwyth hosts the headquarter of the Welsh Pony and Cob Society. Aberystwyth also hosted the first ever Royal Welsh Agricultural Show in 1904.

The town and its locality has been famous for its publishing presses, its booksellers and it also hosts the Books Council of Wales, responsible for promoting Welsh authors, designers, publishers and creating international bridges.

It was in Aberystwyth, following Saunders Lewis' famous radio broadcast in 1962 that Cymdeithas yr Iaith Gymraeg – *the Welsh Language Society* – was formed. This led to the very first mass protest on behalf of the language on Pont Trefechan.

The town's houses of worship have played their part in keeping alive the flames of both the faith and the language. It was in a house in Great Darkgate Street in 1823 that the Methodists Article of Faith was drawn up. And even if some chapels have either closed or united with others, and the Theological College long closed, the two flames still burn.

Aberystwyth also houses the Pantyfedwen Trust, that has done so much in keeping alive the traditional Eisteddfod. There has been internal devolution from Cardiff to Aberystwyth. The Welsh nursery schools movement, Mudiad Meithrin, and the women's society, Merched y Wawr, have their headquarters in the town.

CANOLFAN MERCHED Y WAWR

Agorwyd ar Ddydd Gŵyl Dewi 2000

Aberystwyth, Europe and the World

When you approach Aberystwyth from any direction you will see road signs announcing the town's twinning with Saint-Brieuc in Brittany, a connection that goes back to the late 60s.

The University College naturally plays its international part by attracting students from more than 80 countries. Indeed, the College doesn't stop with internationalism, it has gone interplanetary by designing equipment bound for the surface of Mars.

Aberystwyth and the surrounding area has something for everyone – old and new, urban and rural, fun and learning, local and European, world and interplanetary – Aberystwyth's appeal has no boundaries.

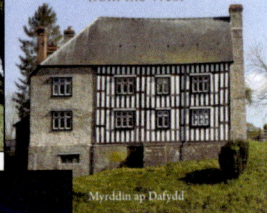

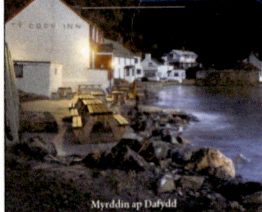

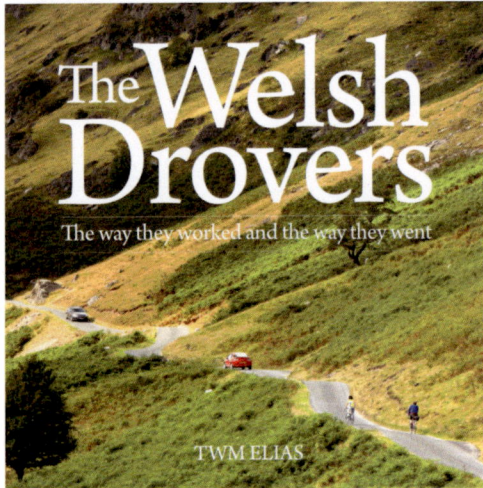